Disclaimer:

The Blackboard training guide was designed for the sole purpose of training based upon the personal coaching and team building of Tiffany Michelle.
We do not guarantee any specific results of private team building.

The Blackboard is not liable for any loss or risk that teams, companies or trainers may incur utilizing
the enclosed material. We guarantee the individual who wants to change will change with focused and consistent efforts in any part of their life.

The Blackboard™
Team Building Training Guide
Copyright©2017

Introduction

Team building can be challenging as you are joining different personalities and skills sets together. Effective teams establish a common goal (what) and purpose (why) at the onset. Which allows you to capitalize on the strengths and uniqueness of each team member, therefore, creating strong and stable individuals effective in any environment.

Your gifts, skills and talents give you an advantage over others, providing a place for you to flourish and dominate. Consequently, manifesting confidence and enormous success for the team. However, this has to be done for everyone on the team and takes time.

If you fail to exercise your gifts and work outside the area(s) of your strengths, you will fail in the long run. Even if you start out strong, the momentum will not last. This will eventually cause you to burn out. Anyone out of place causes problems with productivity and cost the company more money in the long run.

The task of identifying your strengths, unique differences and role is not the sole responsibility of the boss. You are responsible as well. Until everyone on the team is aware of their uniqueness, individuality and put it to use, the team won't reach its full potential. Well placed team members sharpens those around them. They'll never let you slack because they know it will hurt everyone if they do.

This is important because every team is faced with limitations. We all have weaknesses and they can be overcome with the support of the team. Keep in mind too much weight on individual team members

over an extended period of time will cause them to become unstable. Everyone must share the weight to remain strong and stable in challenging environments. This guide will provide some simple tools for becoming a better team member and increasing your personal success.

What you will learn:

- What it means to be a part of a team with a common goal.

- How to use your core strengths to identify your role on the team.

- To operate as a successful team in any environment.

A common goal is essential for team building

A group of people meeting in a certain place at a specific doesn't constitute a team. A team must have a common goal. Webster defines goal as the end toward which effort is directed.

The goal should be the primary reason for the formation of the team. It bonds you together and gives the team purpose. The common goal must be specific, verbalized clearly, and posted for the team to see on a regular basis. To reinforce the goal, repeat it out loud often as a team.

If the team strays away from the established goal, you will fail. The purpose of the goal is to help you focus on why you are there and what you need to accomplish. The goal is like an invisible set of instructions.

It tells you what you should be working toward every day. When every member on the team is confident of the goal and their strengths, you are well on your way to having a strong, successful team.

The common goal should be:

- Specific
- Verbalized clearly
- Posted for the team to see
- Repeated out loud by the team for reinforcement

Notes:

Building a team with purpose

Establishing a common goal for the team allows you to build your team with purpose. The core values of the individual team members should match the core values of the company. During testing seasons, those values and beliefs will be the super glue for keeping the team together.

Any team that is ultimately successful will have similar core values and beliefs. A team is not about any one person, it's about purpose. You're not a good fit for the team unless your values and beliefs match the team's purpose. Everyone on the team should be going in the same direction at all times. The team's effectiveness can be measured by all those who have personally demonstrated the team's goals and purpose.

For example, if the local high school's goal is send every senior to college. A few things must happen first, such as you maintaining your grades, expect to be accepted into college, then apply. When every senior has gone off to college then that team is considered highly successful.

The invisible instructions of the team's goal is providing direction for your life every day. Daily practice of whatever you do develops excellence and excellence pushes you over into greatness.

Developing your core strengths

For the purpose of this training, strengths are defined as defenses, gains, and gifts that provide a return when administered. You may have many strengths, but some stand out more than others. Your core strengths allow you to operate confidently and effortlessly.

Focus your energy on developing your core strengths. They will dramatically increase the value of your work and pay. Be willing to take on new and challenging assignments as long as they allow you to exercise your core strengths.

Notes:

List Three Core Strengths

1. _____

_____

_____

2. _____

_____

_____

3. _____

_____

_____

How Are You Using Your Core Strengths to Help Your Team Succeed? List Them.

1._____
_____
_____

2._____
_____
_____

3._____
_____
_____

Are you having a hard time coming up with three core strengths? For the sake of time, ask the team how you have helped them and you should see a pattern of your strengths.

The key is for you to recognize your core strengths and how you best operate in them. Self-awareness is absolutely necessary in being your best. Your uniqueness gives the team grit and sustainability because it can't be duplicated.

Furthermore, self-awareness prevents comparison or competition within the team. Comparison is evil, you will end up sabotaging the team's efforts if you measure your success by the performance of others.

Let your strengths lead you into your team role

Now that you've established your strengths, are you working in the right role? Use the checklist below to determine.

Signs you're in the right role:

- Able to spot potential problems that others do not see and quickly correct them with ease.

- Efficient in your role and find ways to improve that part of the business or team.

- When challenges arise, you handle them effectively.

- Your creativity level is heighten and it shows in your work.

If you are concerned that you could serve the team better in a different role, schedule a time to talk with the boss. During your meeting, ask to assist or fill in whenever possible in that area. Don't be afraid to let your boss know you believe your strengths are best aligned in another area.

They'll let you know if they agree and would be willing to give it a try. If that doesn't happen, don't become discouraged. Be patient and stay focused. Continue to develop your strengths in your current role. Remain consistent and your strengths will provide a door of opportunity for you sooner or later.

Prepare every day for where you want to be. If it doesn't work out on your current team, something will open elsewhere. Most people fail because they lose focus and perform average or below average work during this time. You should be working even harder now. The average is never promoted, only the excellent.

Notes:

Don't give up if you're not immediately promoted. The true test of your maturity is being your best wherever you are. If you leave before you're ready, you'll be forced to repeat the process. That will set you back even further.

Your time in that position has purpose. The experience you gain is preparing you to move on. It will amaze you how much you'll learn about yourself and others. Your character is being developed for the next level.

When you complete that assignment those doors will automatically close. Allowing the next assignment to find you.

List Ways You Can Personally Improve Your Character

- _____
- _____
- _____
- _____
- _____

Everyday work toward being a better you in these areas. Surround yourself with people who fuel your strengths and keep you accountable.

As we discussed strengths we must also deal with weaknesses.

Your weakness positions you for those you need to connect with in life. If you fight your help, you will never become the individual you were destined to be.

We all have weaknesses and they are designed to push us to reach outside of ourselves for help. Don't run from your weakness. Accept it as necessary to get you where you need to be in life.

List your weakness:

_____

_____

_____

Once you have identified your weakness, ask for help from someone you can trust and that's able to help.

Notes:

Challenging Environments

How do you prepare a team to win in a challenging environment? Create a winning culture. Culture is a way of thinking, behaving, or working that exist in a place or organization according to Webster Dictionary.

The culture is the standard your team expects you to live by. A strong culture provides a model for the team members to carry out. While an unhealthy culture allows everyone to do whatever they want, whenever they want. A team with a strong culture will adapt in adverse environments and succeed.

Keys to Remaining Successful in a Challenging Environment:

- Cultivate a mindset of staying in the moment to minimize your stress level

- Develop strategies for dealing with your weakness in adverse situations.

- Deal with problems immediately

- Eliminate distractions.

- Make it a habit to give your best every day.

Take Action

Make a commitment to take action. Taking action is the fastest way to results. If you don't work your goals, you'll never change or get what you deserve.

Find at least three team members who can help you overcome your weakness with their strengths-skills, talents and gifts.

List them on the action log and what you hope to learn from them and set a deadline for it to be done.

Action Log:

Date: _____
Team Member:_____
Action: _____

_____
_____

Date: _____
Team Member:_____
Action: _____

_____
_____

Date: _____
Team Member:_____
Action: _____

_____
_____

Date: _____
Team Member:_____
Action: _____

_____
_____

Notes:

Notes:

Call It As You See It Group Exercise

Have Someone Read the Instructions Aloud Before You Begin

READY, SET, GO!

You have 10 minutes to perform the total exercise. You can use the time as you would like.

Each member should come up with a name for the team. (Write it in the guide and do not show it to anyone)

After hearing all your team's strengths select someone to guess the team name (they will not be a part of the group task when you all select the team's name). Write their name under team leader in the guide. Select the team's name as a group. You can't select the entry of the team member you selected to receive the information and guess the name.

Sit the team member to receive the information in front of everyone. They can't ask any questions. Nor be involved in the process. The only thing they can request from you is for you to read the description out loud again or describe the picture again. They are allowed to take notes to uncover the name.

Write a description of the team's name without including the team's name itself. Then draw a picture(s) to describe the team's name.

Select a team member to read the description out loud. (You can only read what's written-you can't add anything to it.) Select a team member to describe the picture(s). You can only describe the picture with single words-no sentences allowed.

Team Name

Team Leader

Team Description

Team Picture

Feedback:

Rate the training on a scale of 1 to 5.
(5 being the highest and 1 the lowest.)
       1 2 3 4 5

What did you like about the training?

_____
_____
_____
_____

How can we improve upon the training?

_____
_____
_____
_____

Additional Comments:

_____
_____
_____
_____

www.ingramcontent.com/pod-product-compliance
Lightning Source LLC
Chambersburg PA
CBHW061236180526
45170CB00003B/1329